VOICES OF LONGING

A Contemplation on Being & Belonging

Kingsley L. Dennis

VOICES OF LONGING

A Contemplation on
Being & Belonging

Kingsley L. Dennis

BEAUTIFUL TRAITOR BOOKS

A Few Words

I wrote the content of this small book in a little under three weeks – from February 11th to March 1st 2019, to be precise. It wasn't my intention to write this book, but that's not so important. I had an impulse to scribble some words about longing and belonging in this modern world of ours. The rest just followed. Or rather, I should say they flowed. Then after sixty-four pieces, I felt the flow had come to its natural rest. This is good. What comes, let it come. If it doesn't come naturally, leave it.

I have little more to say on the matter. Perhaps I had nothing to say on the matter in the first place. I was in the right place at the right time, as they say. You are reading the words in this collection exactly as they were first written – there have been no revisions. They arrived, they stayed, and I did not intervene. If they have a life of their own, I can only be thankful.

2nd March 2019

Casa Roja

Andalusia

Let not thy longing be numbed
Let not the voice of thy soul be silent
As we bring the bloom and the seasons
Through the energy of the inner heart.

We live like nomads of the soul, longing for a genuine connection yet wandering through our daily lives without a sense of self, or unity, or relation to the wider world.

We live our lives fragmented, fractured, moving through our days with absent hearts. Life drags us in so many differing directions.

We no longer contemplate – modern life gives us no space. We have no personal sanctuary, no sacred refuge. We kill our time through soulless distractions.

We need to be anchored. Our inherent need to belong – our longing for connection – can be manipulated, or we can be blown in many directions. We need our own essential anchorage.

We are on a lifelong journey from unknowing to knowing, from anonymity to selfhood.

In this world we have a continual sense of belonging to an invisible world – the realm from where we came from.

An invisible umbilical cord attaches us – we feel its pull. This pull is the longing that follows us through-out our lives. We feel it tugging at us, and yet know not what it is.

We live continually on the threshold between the invisible and the visible. We are as solidified ghosts, yearning to find our belonging.

We are wanderers on the threshold. We wish to carve out meaning from the emptiness around us. We indulge in or invent pursuits to substitute for this.

The world is full of people casting lonesome shadows over their lives.

Our lives are populated by visitors. They wander in and out of our landscapes of belonging. They move through our scenarios.

Some stay longer than others. Some we recognize by signs – others are blank faces that leave little residual memory.

We too are our own visitors. Our visit to this realm is never long – or are we interlopers? Trespassers? Are we as invaders on foreign soil?

Our abode here is not fixed – our stay is fleeting. The guests are coming in and wandering through.

The soul is a nomad, wandering both within and without, throughout our lives – some more lost than others. Those who lack an internal wandering mirror this lack in their outer lives. Our interior landscapes require their own roaming.

We step with quiet footsteps. Some leave no trace at all.

The majority of the world is unknown to us – shall remain unknown to us. We step only into so few spaces. Our space becomes an intimate place for us. We are as a stranger to other spaces.

We entered this realm as a stranger. We came with a new face and yet nameless. We were gifted a name that we wore - and which wears us. For some, the name became everything. Who we are became a name. Purpose and meaning were transformed into letters, and their original spaces forgotten.

Many people now belong to their name – are owned by it. They are but its shadow.

Everything in life calls for us to awaken - why do we not awake?

The voice of longing calls out constantly and is drowned by external clutter.

We travelled from afar to come here – we waited a long time for this. A long time to then enter into forgetfulness again.

There is a greatness that sleeps within the human heart. We inhabit our world unawakened, as if marooned, longing for companionship, clinging to confusion.

We are never alone in this realm and yet so many human hearts feel the loneliness.

We listen to the echoes yet seldom do we turn to seek their source.

Each thing, grand or small, is distinctive – we need to be wary of a world that tries to flatten everything out into a copy of itself.

Voices cry in unison – shared opinions become hermetically sealed into a soulless call, whilst the inner voice of distinction sings a delightful harmony that is muffled into static.

Mechanical noise saturates our delicate voices, as it creeps into the in-between spaces, seeping into the crook and crux of our lives - the voice of longing is a natural sound, like water running, birds chirping, the wind rustling, leaves falling...

Dead sounds reverberate throughout this realm –

concrete against asbestos, nylon against plastic, emptiness against urban toxins.

Dead rhythms fall to the tarmac, absorbed into bitumen, crushed under traffic, replaced by horns and sirens.

Our spheres of sensibility slowed to a dull pace, shuddering to a stop – parched and cracked.

Sounds of the soul linger on, eternally, endlessly, forever determined and resolute, awaiting our inner ears to prick up.

We are the sanctuary that our selves long for.

The days and nights that we each live infuses into our bodies – we smell of the similitudes of experience.

Events pull towards us or push away. We jump outside of ourselves to grasp at some social belonging, as a suicide leaps from some empty balcony.

Craving outwards, we push our soul back within, closing the shell. We wear a face of sameness, glaring out, anticipating acknowledgement, pining for recognition. Engage me! – the bland face mourns.

Encouragement is a gift we yearn for. The soul seeks to be recognized for what it is – natural, essential, effervescent, always on and always there.

When you belong to yourself and truly own it, a spark from you can fill an empty house.

Just as a single lighted match dispels the darkness, the light of being dissipates the fear that shreds into our daily lives.

The being is iridescent yet shrouded in contemporary scraps of cloth that we collect to clean our floors.

In a fury we explode ourselves onto the public stage in exasperation to belong. We believe that to be loud is to be strong. To be loud is to belong. Our tribal cries are suppliants to the social gods – 'In this noise I seek entry to thee.' Everyone shouts louder in order to outdo the other – to out-belong the other and climb to the top of the pyramid of social worship. We fail to realize that we fail the gods by leaving ourselves behind. In a fog of urban traffic smoke and pollution we are left standing by the wayside, scrubby faced. The soul sighs. Another time, another time. We become our own furies whilst the soul resides in peace.

To live outside of yourself is to betray who you are.

Longing for affirmation from without – the gentle touch of appreciation, the soft hand on the shoulder, the caring word delivered.

We seek the attainable from without making it unattainable.

Letters flow and then freeze as stalactites before the word has been brought.

Utterances lie crestfallen, debris scattered across the playground, dishevelled toys as rags.

The wilderness lies without.

Belonging recognizes belonging in another.

When you stop fighting for it, the belonging will come.

The more you rush towards it, the more it fades away.

True belonging has no name yet is here to stay.

It heeds the call of a joyful longing.

It knocks on the door and enters from within.

First feel your belonging as a private space. Intimate. Sheltered. Safe and secure. Hold this belonging with light hands. Then let it go and feel how it remains clasped tight to you. It sings with your resonance. It dances to your tune. You both recognize each other intimately like bardo lovers. Breath through each other, breathing into one. This belonging is your very being. There never was anything else.

Your unrest is your mirror. The conventions that stifle you are your reflection.

Gather them in. Count them. Assort through the coloured stones. See the signs of your disentanglement.

The scenes shake before you as a movie shot from unsteady hands.

Take up all these fragments and own them. Take them into you – let them hang upon your interior tree where the branches root through your body and soul.

And say YES…I accept me.

It is said that the word desire comes from the form 'de-sidus,' meaning 'away from a star.' Our desires take us away from our own star, from the glare of luminosity into façades of splintered filaments. Distracting desires take us away from the source of our soul – our nuclear burning engine of self. We are thrown into dark matter and entangled with the globules, the spluttering of choked exhaust fumes.

Only genuine desire takes us back through the Ariadne's thread to our star-being, where we belong.

We long for the eternal nebulae that cradles our journey, embryonic and unfolding in innocence.

Our minds hang heavy with the over there –

we are away from ourselves. Looking back over our shoulders for our presence. We see footprints from some path we have walked and yet were strangely absent. Our minds cast afar in other places.

Our attention caught within the vices of the modern carnival. Now we are over there, someplace else. We forget where we last stood. We have no markers. Our presence flaps in the breeze and bends to the erratic rhythms pounded out by entrapment in a conventional everyday. We are swallowed by the everyday, our energy eaten, consumed by others. We long to return to where we once stood. Where our footsteps once trod. To those markers we must have left behind – someplace. We seek our presence in the corners and do not see the very thing which we embody, and which ensouls us.

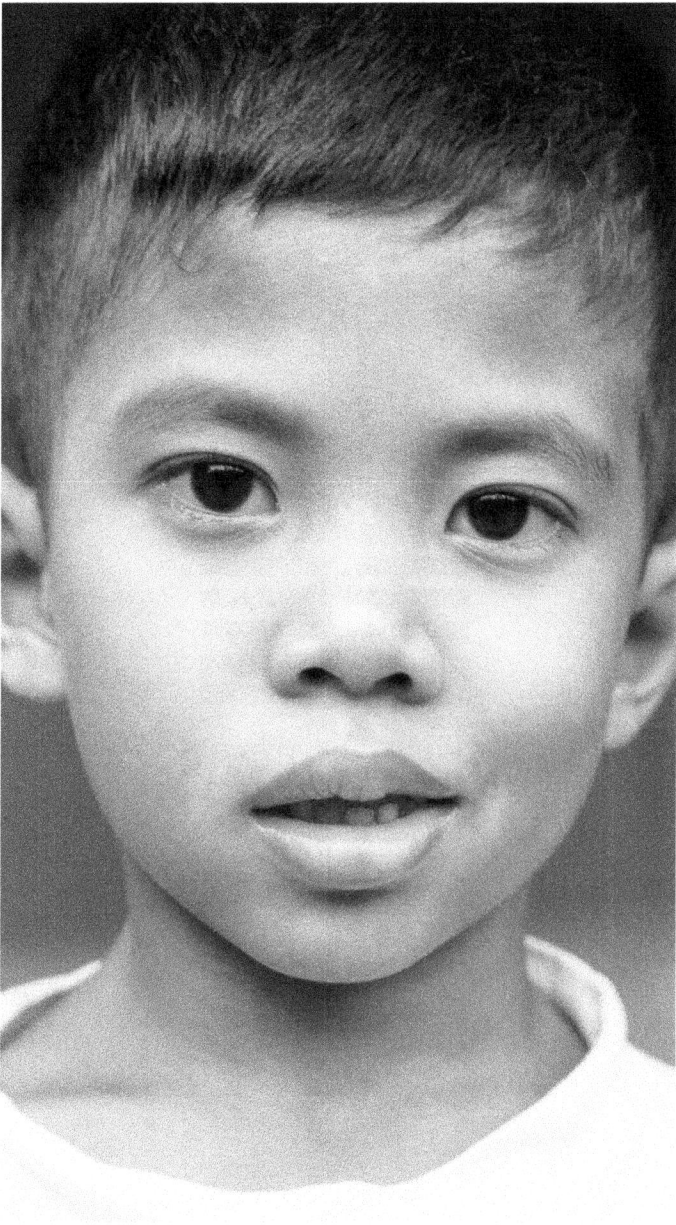

The soul longs for the infinite, so the system throws out the finite – finite objects to entice and delight, for our hands to wrap around, squeeze on tight.

The infinite is abstract, not quite knowable – why chase this when we can have the tangible?

Belonging fed on consumables. Longing unquenched. The waiting lasts for a very long time.

The frontier of the infinite is absorbed into everything. We only fail to see.

Reach out by reaching within. There are no obstacles, only false brigands.

We grew out of the invisible world. We slipped into form. We grabbed at the world around us. We wrapped ourselves in these outer garments. We declared ourselves anew. And the threads that bind us to the invisible themselves became invisible.

We strut as warriors when in truth we are but puppets. Our strings are tied by external hands whilst the threads that connect our hearts lay fallow.

This is the longing that tugs at us constantly. We pull away by our puppet strings. We run while standing still. Going nowhere we throw our time away. The puppet play consumes us. The invisible world envelops us…and waits, eternally, infinitely.

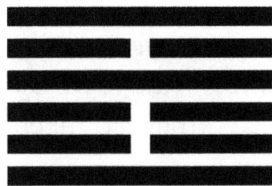

There is a landscape where I wish to meet my longing. If I pull hard enough, perhaps she will respond. Or what if we are at both ends of a rope and we are both pulling? Like a tug-of-war we are pulling in a direction that is for one, not both.

Longing – can we not be unified? Are we not yearning for the same?

The same sound of a bird's cry, a wind's passing, a tree's rustling?

Longing replies: the heart is one. It encompasses everything. Why do you seek the outside of it when there is none?

Fool and fools. Deaf mutants. We think we're listening when we're only telling our own side of the story.

To belong we must not have borders. We cannot close down, block, close-off. Our choices must always lead to opening of something new.

The old will close of its own accord.

Our experiences map a pattern for us that the soul sees clearly. Such patterns are a projection from the inner landscape.

Observe their curves, their lines. They are wishing to tell us something. Until we can see, our blindness is bound to the labyrinth carved at our feet.

Be faithful to your longing. Do not make it into a common arrangement, a dutiful compromise. Your longing is not a convention to be housed. It is not an appointment to be kept, a schedule, a psychiatric sofa to lounge upon. Your longing is an immensity. It reaches out for your participation, your full-blooded energy. It wants to dance. It wants to rise up like a geyser and shoot out like spray. Do not define it or place it in a box at night to sleep. Do not ask if it wishes to go for a walk. Run – and it will run with you. Dance – and it will dance with you. It is not your shadow nor your partner though. It is embedded not attached. It knows but does not tell. It calls but does not speak. It lives but does not breath. It is exactly where it cannot be found, and nowhere where it is not. It is that. Long for it.

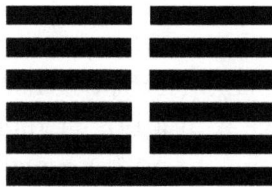

Longing is the primordial tapping.
Tap. Tap. Tap.

It is vital. It is vitality. It's what keeps you burning away without you knowing it.

Did you never stop to think why? Or give thanks?

It has never asked anything from you except your self. Could you not give this? What are you holding back when you cloud this longing?

Even if you go and climb the Himalayas   you will escape nothing. Everything travels with you.

Why be absent at the peak of a mountain when you could be full?

Longing will pinch at you wherever you are.

It will be announced.

You can call it by other names. You can baptize it by blood, water, and wine – yet it knows who you are. You can dress it up in glad rags and brand names, and yet nothing shall be different. You can spend a lifetime being in any other place rather than the here. You will have gone nowhere. Wherever you travel you are within the same space. The exterior scenery moves, like cardboard backdrops at some school play. Everything else stays where it is. Where it has ever been. Do you know how to touch the ever been?

You should.

Meaning is its own centre of longing.
Significance for being here.
What do we do – and why?

Shuffling as bodies through our daily labours. We march from one project to the next. We race to deadlines. We meet those deadlines – or not. We accomplish small tasks. We get rewarded. Some praise. A trickle of reputation. A slap on the back. A shout down when we fail at someone else's task that they landed onto us. We panic at what other people may think or say of us. We do other's bidding so we can spend their pay check.

Significance for being here.
What do we do – and why?
Meaning is its own centre of longing.

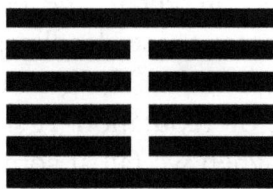

The modern world leans in and closes around us to domesticate our hearts. Our minds are shaped by society's phantasms. Invisible hands sculpture thoughts into our heads.

Nature is wild and beckons to us to come forth into her arms. We belong also to the soil, the sounds, the textures of Nature. We belong to the wind, to the rain, to the rays of the sun.

We long for warmth and the encompassing embrace. Yet our domesticated hearts often pull us away. Back into rooms, behind walls, between programs. We curl back into our personas and smile at the doormen, the salespeople, the labcoats, and the invisible hands.

We long for ourselves.

Our lives are streamlined into disinherited
segments.
We've been denied the roots of our legacy.
You know when you've been cheated
Because of the taste in your mouth.

Shelves filled with mouth fresheners and perfumes
to provide the perfect cover-up. A crime has been
committed and we're investing in our own clean-
up.

The soul observes from the side-lines, taking notes.

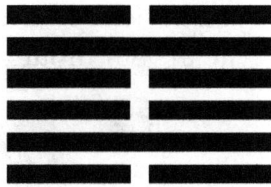

Don't be prisoner or prison guard.
Don't deny yourself your freedom.
Walk towards to meet yourself.
Wipe away your social face,
your conventional graces

And greet yourself as if for the first time.

There's no use in longing for a god if you can't first find the god in you.

We chase after secondary substitutes like precious birds chasing the light.

Our societies are lonesome engines churning out saccharine belongings. We play the prison guards to our own prisons. We have our own logic of concealment. We guard the portals to our inner mansion with conventions of the public face.

There's no use longing for some touch of grace if you can't first find the grace in you.

Ready-made belonging. Packaged at birth. Provided by our institutions. Sanctioned by the state.

Belonging in a box. Standard size that fits most all. We wear it as a jacket or as an overall.

A multitude of belongings. Billions of them banging against each other – banging into borders and bumping into walls. Belongings wrapped in bubble-coats bouncing down the road. Belongings trapped in avatars and belongings languishing in dreams.

Ready-made but never right.
Easy given but never truly yours.
Belonging to your true belonging is the haunting
Call that cries out to you from your first breath.

Routine and repetition dulls and anesthetizes the soulful longing to belong and to love.

Our hearts are sanctuaries that birth the precious light.

Our lives condemn us to noise and sacrifice, yearning for the mystery that reveals itself within the deepest moment of the darkest night.

Unknown to ourselves, we miss our own most intimate belongings. We wash away our inner sight through daily rituals, repeated in the dead mind. Half-aware of the other world, of the invisible hand that graces us with a fleeting touch. Half-present in our minds - half-present in our lives. Only there long enough to buy the souvenir. One eye open to say to others that we're awake. One eye open to fool the world. Yet it is the world that fools us. And we are the janitors with one-eye closed.

Despite the eternal distances we are standing in the same place. Destinations wait like empty altars for our own arrival.

You have to take your longing and own it – it must be yours, right down to the body's bone. Right down to the spirit's soul.

And when you truly own it, your longing will take you along. Along for the ride, along for the game. Along for the love – a love that is never tame.

Until you can belong to your longing, those empty altars will continue to wait in vain.

Destinations have always been inside of us – glad that we came.

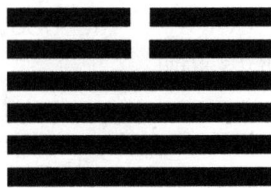

Longing brought me here to see you. It wanted me to see if you were human. If you had experienced loneliness; if you knew the taste of life and loss. If you knew fear and trepidation, anxiety and calm. If you were real behind the eyes, beating within the heart, racing in the blood, and aching in the bones. It wanted me to tell you it's okay to be quiet and not to speak. That it's normal to be tired and that you don't have to smile if you don't wish to. That it's okay to be you, no matter what you hear or see from others. That there's a sanctuary within your soul and a voice that sings to you that no-one else can hear. It wanted me to watch you as you listen to these words. And it wanted me to disappear the moment you felt me near.

I cannot claim you.

True longing knows how to break things down in order to place them back again. This is the art of assemblage. Of knowing how wholes cannot be analysed into tiny separate parts. Longing is a dust cloud composed of diamonds that makes a shawl of finest sand dunes.

Sand is not the shards of rough-cut struggle but the soft carpet that bare feet love to walk upon.

Longing has many faces yet belonging only has one.

The ways in which we long, out-do us as through trial and error we grasp at ways to belong.

Seeking confirmation we split ourselves into a myriad of social faces, through which each one we thread our longing.

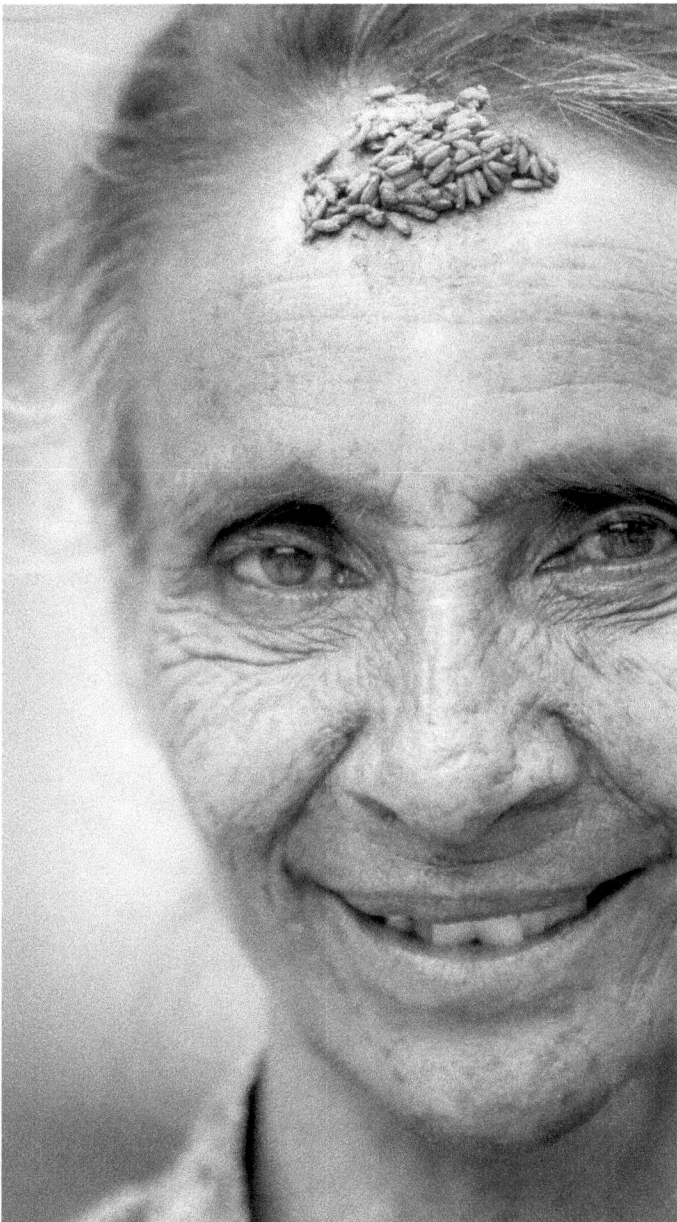

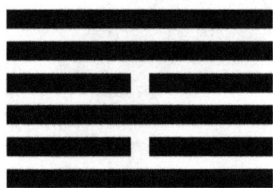

If you engage with the emptiness it will not engulf you
if you are deep rooted within.

Emptiness is a bore hole for those who have not found their ground and experienced their own well of hidden treasures.

Emptiness is a peaceful silence, a safe haven, for those who belong to themselves.

And it is a fathomless void for those devoid and hidden from their internal connection.

We burden ourselves through our own conventions, placing barrier upon barrier, building up our playground until the walls are too far to see.

We throw in our bones of suffering, to feel an intricate kind of pain that gnaws from within.

We create our masks of pretension to hide the fibre of our soul – then we go wandering, wondering why we cannot find what we thought we had all along.

The sounds within us speak with their own voices.

No longing is ever silent for too long. No wound is ever invisible forever. No healing is ever absent from our lives.

We are never far away when we've always been so close.

Every life has its secret structure.
Every life carries itself as a benediction.

Every breath is an ancient longing.
Every breath touches the threshold of the soul.

Every forgiveness is a blessing upon the self.
Every forgiveness is communion with the common
heart.

Humanity is the heart of its own secret structure.

Sometimes we try to evade that which we long to attain.

The love of longing acts as the longing of love.

There is nothing outside of our belonging in life or in death.

We move between the different sides of the same eternity, catching glimpses of our shadows and our flame. Catching glimpses of our home and the way we came. We remain unsure despite our hidden goal. Sometimes we try to evade that which we long to attain.

What does it mean to be your own living presence?
Or to become your own living presence? What
does 'being' mean?

Throw away the words. Throw away the song.
Don't follow any longing.

Just belong.

Be.

B...

Living wall-to-wall leaves no space to 'be.' We are touching all sides of the box in which we believe we are free. Why don't we try living more with the crooked lines, the wobbly walls? Instead, we are so engrossed with the concrete; so entangled with the unseen cables that tie us down in new, modern contortions.

We have divided our being into regions. In these regional spaces very little belongs to anything or anyone. Everything is abstract, like a nameless song…like these dispossessed words.

The mystery has no colour.

The wonder has no smell.

Yet blessing has a taste.

And gratitude has a whisper, that echoes like a soul singing from its shell.

Lyricism has slowly been lost from our world. It is being replaced by the arrogance of the text-as-fact. Wonder is hardening back into the wheel. Awe is evaporating into the winter fog. Taking our breath away is now a thievery of the air. Everything is waiting for you now – are You coming out?

Are You there?

There comes a time when things that belong in your life no longer fit.

It's as if they've suddenly come lose and nothing is able to gel them together again.

So you have to wonder - did they ever belong to you?

You have to ask yourself – did they ever really fit?

Or were you just squeezing them into tight places and telling yourself that everything belonged just as it should?

Despite the allure of magic, the modern world races towards domestication of all finer things. Despite all the assurances otherwise, the modern corporeal body wishes the inner longing to be trained by the clock. In time, all things will adhere to time – and the mystery of being will have missed its appointment.

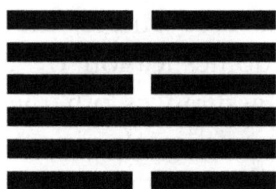

Your words shall reach others – even when you don't speak them. Because what lies behind the words also belong to you. And what lies beyond your belonging is shared amongst others too. Longing is like an island that dissolves into being...and then into BE...finally into ONE. Then everything is gone.

We belong to the cosmos. We belong to the stars.

We belong to the firmament. We belong to the foundation.

We belong because we always have. We didn't go anywhere – we just forgot. And then we forgot to remember. And then we forgot to ask why. We don't have to do anything, apart from opening our eyes.

Then love comes, and longing goes.

Our shadow also belongs to us. We need to absorb it into us fully before we can fully belong to ourselves.

Without our shadow we remain shallow. Our longing remains shallow, and in its naivety, it clings to social media tribes that hang around in dubious spaces. Such tribes attract one to another in an attempt to create gravity through a collective of levity. Seek your own depth, your own weight. Be heavy in yourself – you do not need to rely on the accumulation of lightness to bring you some gravitas. It is already within you – heavier than the densest meteorite.

Gravitate towards your own rock.

In our fast-track feeling of need - of wanting - to belong to the world, we have sought out the substitutes for our belonging – a perversion of our true needs. We have been drawn out of ourselves by unnecessary twenty-first century distractions. Drawn away from our own recesses of self-examination and out into the bright and brassy light of days...

...days of amusements and feel-good factors that polish our exterior coats yet neglect the shadows that the soul casts within.

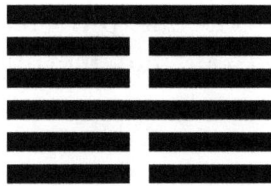

We have forgotten what makes us well. We have become wrapped within the flare of our modern cultures. Our sense of belonging has become warped. It has created an illusion of connection that is superficial and under nourishes.

It is we who exile our self from ourselves.

We long for the departed. We long for the now. An absence of yesterday. A seeking for today. There is nowhere to go. There is everywhere to stay.

We take many roads seeking for a destination. Not knowing that we shall never arrive for we have not learned how to begin.

We are the beginning and the eternal.
We are the contradiction and the paradox.
We are the straight line and the curve.

We are here to form a middle.

In belonging to our ego, we have become absent from the earth. It's like choosing to be intimate with the wrong friend. A loyalty broken. A fractured friendship.

These are diversions we live within. Diversions that hide the one we love. We love our substitutes instead. Loving them brings some release, a warm bed.

In this absence we become vulnerable to real presence. A stranger to the centre of ourselves.

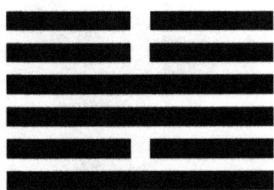

Our social worlds are sophisticated structures of absence. They speak through a grammar of separation, of unknowing. They teach us not to know ourselves – to be absent within the many. Social belonging is a gel that holds the superficial in orbit. We revolve in these empty orbits like neutrons, without charge, without the positive energy. This is the belonging we need to break away from. We need to seek attraction to other orbits. Orbits of longing and love, where the positive vibration holds us in unity.

We are slowly changing the orbits of the twenty-first century world.

Modern life cherishes the external. This is the land of ghosts, of alluring phantasms that speak in tongues. This is the land of manufactured dreams and fabricated fantasies. This is the land that divides us into parts and sells those parts back to us. It is the land of no-win negotiation where the soul lands in debt and the heart is traded for a dime-store mystery.

This is not the land where the grass sings sweetly.

Let us not talk ourselves out of being ourselves. Let us not talk ourselves out of the way. We are in the middle of the way for a very good reason. We are over there and also here for a very good reason.

Now go – find that reason.

When the old shelters are gone, taken away – where will you find refuge? If you don't have it now – when and how?

You need to go where you haven't been before. The signs will be different. There are no signs. There are some signs, but you won't recognize them. The signs have been painted over or recycled into fake trees for lining the interior of shopping malls. When your words no longer have fluency, you will fall over them. Will you allow yourself to be tripped up like this? Have you learnt how to bend down carefully and scoop up your fallen words and to plant them by the wayside?

If you don't yet have this refuge – what will you do? What will you do when you turn around and you can no longer find yourself? Have you learnt how to meet yourself for the first time?

If not, you should start now.

There is no place for exile. It is for refugees. Refugees of the self crowd-out this no-place. Outcasts from some place. Belonging, longing, and being all come together in exile.

We are a species in exile. Have you ever thought about this? What it means?

If you do not consider yourself in exile, you have not spoken with your soul lately.

Longing is poetry. It is visionary. It is not public property. It does not belong in boardrooms or at the stock exchange. It does not make deals or shake hands. It does not renegotiate its terms or lease itself out.

Longing is an immense power. It blows through the body and engulfs you. It shimmers all around. It bangs on drums and whistles like a flock of migrating birds coming home to their nests. It sits on your head and laughs. It slides into the heart and sighs. It joins up with the soul and sings.

Longing is not fractured, like the world.

They say that we now belong to the instant – yet it seems to be more the instant of forgetfulness. We belong more to lost memories than remembrance.

Belonging to an old world will take us nowhere. This is like a stroll through a deserted village where the people have fled. The walls have begun to crumble. The church bells were stolen long ago. There was a prayer written on a piece of paper and stuffed into a niche...

yet it blew away upon the breeze. It calls out from yonder. It has settled in a hedgerow close to where a new settlement will arise.

Will you follow it?

Longing is a language, longing is a song.

Longing is a soul in rags that's as glorious as the sun when it kisses the early birds that arise to greet it.

Longing wishes to belong to nothing beyond its own song. For there is none.

We are afraid of becoming our own outcasts. We may feel the periphery is cold and uninviting. We have been led to believe in this. We have been compelled to seek the social centre. Yet the real centre is within You. Whether this lies at the social periphery or not is irrelevant. When you are in your own centre you are everywhere. Seek your own centre first, and then enjoy the freedom.

No institution should place a hand or a shadow over your longing or your eternal right 'to be.'

'I am' is the right to belong to the Me and Thee. It is formless and forever. It has come from everything and nothing and shall return to All and nothing.

In-between time, learn to nurture the All of yourself.

It is your adventure – embrace the beauty of it.

Beautiful Traitor Books was founded in 2012 as an independent print-on-demand imprint to provide unusual and inspiring books for the discerning reader.

Our books are works that delve into various domains whether it is books for children, science fiction, social affairs, philosophy, theatre plays, or poetry. All the books we publish seek to explore innovative and creative ideas. Many of them also tell a good story - stories that have different perspectives on life and on the human condition.

Beautiful Traitor Books is not only about offering the reader entertainment. We also seek to offer something that is like a nutrition; something of value that the reader can take away from the book. Good books function on more than one level. Put simply, we thrive on books that have the capacity to shift the reader.

Come and join the conversation – find out more at: www.beautifultraitorbooks.com

www.ingramcontent.com/pod-product-compliance
Lightning Source LLC
Chambersburg PA
CBHW060255050426
42448CB00009B/1646